STEP-BY-STEP

Indian Side Dishes

STEP-BY-STEP

Indian Side Dishes

CARA HOBDAY

SHOOTING STAR PRESS

This edition printed in 1995 for:
Shooting Star Press Inc
230 Fifth Avenue – Suite 1212
New York, NY 10001

Shooting Star Press books are available at special discounts for bulk purchases for sales promotions, premiums, fund-raising, or educational use. Special edition or book excerpts can also be created to specification. For details contact: Special Sales Director, Shooting Star Press Inc., 230 Fifth Avenue, Suite 1212, New York, NY 10001

ISBN 1-57335-003-6

Produced by Haldane Mason, London

Printed in Italy

Acknowledgements:
Art Direction: Ron Samuels
Editor: Joanna Swinnerton
Series Design: Pedro & Frances Prá-Lopez / Kingfisher Design
Page Design: Somewhere Creative
Photography: Joff Lee
Styling: John Lee Studios
Home Economist: Cara Hobday

Photographs on pages 6, 20, 34, 48 & 62 are reproduced by permission of
ZEFA Picture Library (UK) Ltd.

Note:
Cup measurements in this book are for American cups. Tablespoons are assumed to be 15ml. Unless otherwise stated, milk is assumed to be full-fat, eggs are AA extra large and pepper is freshly ground black pepper.

Contents

CHAPTER ONE

Soups & Appetizers

As in the rest of Asia, all the dishes in an Indian meal are usually served at once, rather than in separate courses. However, as some people may prefer to eat Indian food in a Western style, and begin with an appetizer of some kind, I have included a selection of tasty morsels here. The Spicy Bites in this section are exactly the kind of thing that one might nibble with drinks on a social visit, or while the main course of an Indian meal is being prepared.

Many of these dishes would also be ideal for taking on a picnic, a favorite Indian family pastime. A common Sunday activity is to take a picnic to the town "maidan" or green space and spend a lazy afternoon with family and friends chatting, eating and snoozing, and maybe throwing a few cricket balls at a makeshift wicket!

Opposite: The unmistakable profile of the Taj Mahal.

STEP 1

STEP 4

STEP 4

STEP 5

CUCUMBER & TOMATO SOUP

This chilled soup is not an authentic Indian dish, but makes a delicious appetizer. It could also be served between courses as a "cooler," which might be welcomed by those unaccustomed to hot spices.

SERVES 6

4 tomatoes, peeled and deseeded
3 pounds watermelon, seedless if available
4-inch piece English cucumber, peeled and deseeded
2 scallions, green part only, chopped
1 tbsp chopped fresh mint
salt and pepper
fresh mint sprigs to garnish

1 Cut 1 tomato into ½-inch dice.

2 Remove the rind from the watermelon, and remove the seeds if it is not seedless.

3 Put the 3 remaining tomatoes into a blender or food processor, and, with the motor running, add the cucumber, scallion and watermelon. Blend until smooth.

4 If not using a food processor, push the deseeded watermelon through a sieve (strainer). Chop the cucumber, scallion and the 3 remaining tomatoes finely and add to the melon.

5 Stir the diced tomatoes and mint into the melon mixture. Check for seasoning. Chill overnight, then check for seasoning again. Transfer to a serving dish, and serve, garnished with mint sprigs.

INSTANT SOUP

Although this soup does improve if chilled overnight, it is also delicious as a quick appetizer to whip up just before a meal, and serve immediately.

STEP 1

STEP 3

STEP 3

STEP 4

BITE-SIZED BAJEES

Don't be surprised at the shape these form – they are odd, but look good when arranged on a tray with the yogurt dipping sauce. They make an ideal snack to serve with pre-dinner cocktails.

MAKES 20

2 heaped tbsp gram flour (garbanzo bean
    flour)
$^1/_2$ tsp turmeric
$^1/_2$ tsp cumin seeds, ground
1 tsp garam masala
pinch of cayenne
1 egg
1 large onion, quartered and sliced
1 tbsp chopped fresh cilantro
3 tbsp bread crumbs (optional)
oil for deep-frying
salt

SAUCE:
1 tsp coriander seeds, ground
1$^1/_2$ tsp cumin seeds, ground
1 cup natural yogurt
salt and pepper

1 Put the gram flour into a large bowl, and mix in the spices. Make a well in the center, and add the egg. Stir to form a gluey mixture. Add the onion, and sprinkle on a little salt. Add the cilantro and stir. If the mixture is not stiff enough, add the bread crumbs.

2 Heat the oil for deep-frying over a medium heat until hot – a cube of bread should brown in it in 30 seconds.

3 Push a teaspoonful of the mixture into the oil with a second teaspoon to form fairly round balls. The bajees should firm up quite quickly. Cook in batches of 8–10. Keep stirring them, so that they brown evenly. Drain on plenty of paper towels, and keep them warm in the oven until ready to serve.

4 To make the sauce, roast the spices in a skillet. Remove from the heat, and stir in the yogurt. Season well.

USING HOT OIL

Make sure that the pan and all the utensils are properly dried before use. Do not let any water come into contact with the hot oil, or the oil will spit and splutter, which could be dangerous.

STEP 1

STEP 2

STEP 3

STEP 4

CORONATION SALAD

I have based this on a dish called Coronation Chicken, which was invented to celebrate Queen Victoria's coronation as a symbol of Anglo-Indian links, and is still popular today. This version uses shrimp instead of chicken.

SERVES 4

1 red bell pepper
$^1/_3$ cup golden raisins
1 celery stalk, sliced
$^3/_4$ cup corn
1 sharp, green dessert apple, diced
1 cup green seedless grapes, washed and
   halved
$1^1/_2$ cups cooked basmati rice
$^1/_2$ cup cooked, peeled shrimp (optional)
1 romaine lettuce, washed and drained
1 tsp paprika to garnish

DRESSING:
4 tbsp mayonnaise
2 tsp mild curry powder
1 tsp lemon juice
1 tsp paprika
pinch of salt

1 Deseed and chop the red bell pepper.

2 Combine the golden raisins, red bell pepper, celery, corn, apple and grapes in a large bowl. Stir in the rice, and shrimp if using.

3 Put all the dressing ingredients into a small bowl, and whisk them vigorously.

4 Pour the dressing over the salad, and mix well.

5 Line the serving plate with romaine lettuce leaves, and spoon on the salad. Sprinkle over the paprika, and serve.

MAYONNAISE

Mayonnaise can be bought in varying thicknesses, from the type that you spoon out of the jar to the pouring variety. If you need to thin down mayonnaise for a dressing, simply add water little by little until the desired consistency is reached.

12

STEP 2

STEP 3

STEP 4

STEP 5

SAMOSAS

I first encountered this recipe in a Fijian-Indian restaurant in Sydney. In order to quell our hunger as we waited for our food, we were served with these memorable tuna samosas. Each filling recipe makes enough to fill all the pastry.

MAKES 32

DOUGH:
4 cups all-purpose flour
$^1/_2$ tsp turmeric
$^1/_2$ tsp salt
scant $^1/_2$ cup ghee
scant 1 cup milk, mixed with a little lemon
  juice

TUNA FILLING:
$^1/_2$ tsp each of turmeric and cayenne
1 tsp ground cumin
1 tsp ground coriander
7-ounce can of tuna, drained
$^1/_3$ cup frozen peas, cooked
$^1/_2$ cup diced boiled potatoes
salt and pepper

VEGETARIAN FILLING:
8 ounces white potatoes, boiled
$^1/_2 \times$ 14-ounce can of artichoke hearts,
  drained and puréed
1 tsp black pepper, ground
2 tsp coriander seeds, ground
1 tsp cumin seeds, ground
$^1/_2$ tsp fenugreek seeds, ground
2 large tomatoes, peeled and deseeded
$^1/_2$ cup frozen peas, cooked

SAUCE:
6 anchovies
2 tbsp natural yogurt

1 To make the dough, sift the flour, turmeric and salt into a bowl. Rub in the ghee. Add enough milk to form a fairly soft dough. Cover and set aside.

2 To make the tuna filling, roast the spices in a large skillet. Remove from the heat, and add the tuna, peas and potatoes. Stir well, and season. Continue from step 4.

3 To make the vegetarian filling, mash the potatoes, and combine with the artichokes. Roast the spices in a large skillet. Remove from the heat, and add the potato mixture. Stir well to combine. Chop the tomatoes, and carefully fold in with the peas. Season.

4 Roll out the dough, and cut out 16 5-inch rounds. Cut each round in half, and put a teaspoonful of filling on each half.

5 Brush the edges with milk, and fold each half over to form a triangle. Seal well, and crimp the edges. Bake in a preheated oven at 375°F.

6 To make the sauce, mash the anchovies, then mix with the yogurt and season. Serve with the hot samosas.

STEP 1: Nuts

STEP 2: Nuts

STEP 2: Mussels

STEP 3: Mussels

SPICY BITES

Here are three delicious morsels to whet the appetite before a meal. Use zucchini with the flowers still attached, if you can find them. If zucchini isn't your favorite vegetable, most other vegetables taste just as good deep-fried, so try anything you like.

SERVES 4

SPICED NUTS:
1 cup mixed nuts, such as peanuts, cashews
    and blanched almonds
1 dried red chili
1 tsp sunflower oil
1 garlic clove
1/2 tsp salt
1 tsp garam masala
1/2 tsp clear honey

1 Cook the nuts in a dry, heavy-bottomed pan over moderate heat until the oil comes off, about 5 minutes.

2 Add the remaining ingredients except the honey, and cook for an additional 3 minutes, stirring frequently. Add the honey, and cook for 2 minutes.

3 Remove from the heat, transfer to a serving dish and serve.

MUSSEL MORSELS:
2 pounds small mussels, scrubbed
3 tbsp mayonnaise
1 tsp garam masala
1/2 red chili, deseeded and finely chopped
2 scallions, finely chopped
3/4 cup white bread crumbs
salt

1 Put a little water in the bottom of a large pan. Discard any mussels that are not firmly closed. Add the mussels, and cover the pan. Set over a high heat, and leave for 5 minutes; do not uncover.

2 Drain the mussels, and discard any unopened ones. Remove the shells, and reserve.

3 Chop the mussel meat finely. Stir the mayonnaise into the mussel meat. Add the remaining ingredients and season to taste. Spoon the mixture back into the shells, and arrange on a plate.

DEEP-FRIED ZUCCHINI
1 cup all-purpose flour
1/2 tsp each turmeric and cayenne
2/3 cup water
2 eggs
vegetable oil
1 zucchini, cut into batons

1 Sift the flour and spices together, Add the water, eggs and 1 tablespoon oil. Whisk until smooth.

2 Heat some oil in a wok. Dip the batons into the batter, and drop into the oil. When evenly cooked, remove and drain on paper towels.

STEP 1

STEP 2

STEP 3

STEP 4

BUTTERFLY PRAWNS

These prawns look stunning when presented on the skewers, and they will certainly be an impressive prelude to the main meal.

Serves 2–4

8 wooden skewers

16 raw tiger prawns, shelled, leaving tails
   intact
juice of 2 limes
1 tsp cardamom seeds
2 tsp cumin seeds, ground
2 tsp coriander seeds, ground
1/2 tsp ground cinnamon
1 tsp ground turmeric
1 garlic clove, crushed
1 tsp cayenne
2 tbsp oil
cucumber slices to garnish

1 Soak 8 wooden skewers in water for 20 minutes. Cut the prawns lengthways in half down to the tail, so that they flatten out to a symmetrical shape.

2 Thread a prawn on to 2 wooden skewers, with the tail between them, so that, when laid flat, the skewers hold the prawn in shape. Thread another 3 prawns on to these 2 skewers in the same way. Repeat until you have 4 sets of 4 prawns each.

3 Lay the skewered prawns in a non-porous, non-metallic dish, and sprinkle over the lime juice.

4 Combine the spices and the oil, and coat the prawns well in the mixture.

5 Cover and chill for 4 hours.

6 Cook over a hot barbecue or in a broiler pan lined with foil under a preheated broiler for 6 minutes, turning once.

7 Serve immediately, garnished with cucumber and accompanied by a sweet chutney – walnut chutney is ideal.

RAW PRAWNS OR SHRIMP

When marinating or stir-frying with prawns or shrimp, try to use the raw ones, as they will take up the flavors in the dish that you are cooking. They are widely available frozen, and sometimes fresh from a fish vendor.

CHAPTER TWO

Vegetables

After an Indian meal, whether I am eating it in India or in a restaurant elsewhere or somebody's home, I'm usually left longing for a little greenery, salad, or crunchy vegetables after so many rich sauces and cooked dishes. So I have included here a few options to balance your Indian meal with some vegetable dishes. If your main meal consists of a meat with sauce, such as Rogan Josh or Tikka Masala, try accompanying it with the Kashmiri Spinach or the deliciously simple Spicy Cauliflower. For a dry tandoori or Biryani, try pairing it with the Eggplant Curry for a balanced meal.
The Eggplant Bhaji, a dry curry dish, could be paired with a lentil dish for a simple meal, as could other vegetable and dal dishes.

The flavors of a bhaji are hidden in the very small amount of sauce that you are left with at the end of the cooking time, so do not be deceived into thinking that as there is no sauce, there is no flavor.

Opposite: *A fruit market is held by the side of a canal in southern India.*

EGGPLANT BHAJI

The panch poran spice mix used here is one of the many traditional spice mixes used in Indian cooking, and originated in the Bengal state. To make the spice mix, use 2 tsp whole cumin seeds, 2 tsp black mustard seeds, 2 tsp fennel seeds, ³⁄₄ tsp fenugreek and 1 tsp onion seeds.

STEP 1

STEP 2

STEP 3

STEP 4

SERVES 4

2 tbsp mustard oil
4 tbsp sunflower oil
1 tsp panch poran spice mix (see above)
6 baby eggplants, quartered, or 2 eggplants,
    cut into 1-inch cubes
¹⁄₄ tsp cayenne
1 tsp coriander seeds, ground
¹⁄₂ tsp turmeric
7-ounce can of chopped tomatoes in juice
¹⁄₂ tsp sugar
2 tsp lime juice
salt

1 Heat the mustard oil in a wok or large skillet until it just starts to smoke. Reduce the heat, and add the sunflower oil. Add the panch poran mix to the pan. Stir once, and add all the eggplant.

2 Add the cayenne, coriander and turmeric, and stir over a high heat for 2–3 minutes until the eggplant is sealed on all sides.

3 Add the chopped tomatoes and their juice to the pan and bring to the boil.

4 Simmer for 15 minutes, or until the bhaji is nearly dry. Stir once or twice. Remove from the heat, and stir in the sugar, a pinch of salt and the lime juice.

5 Transfer to a warmed serving dish, and serve immediately.

EGGPLANTS

Most Asian cooks do not salt eggplants, and I don't either. The eggplants that we get for most of the year are so fresh that they do not have any bitter juices, especially the plump, shiny ones that have been left on the plant until they are sweet, and immediately transported to the point of sale – the old-fashioned practise of picking unripe produce and letting it ripen on the ship is not so common now, due to modern growing methods.

STEP 1

STEP 2

STEP 3

STEP 4

CURRIED ROAST POTATOES

This is the kind of Indian-inspired dish that would fit easily into any Western menu. Delicious on a buffet, or a surprise accompaniment to a traditional roast dinner – or how about serving with a curry in place of the more traditional rice?

SERVES 4

2 tsp cumin seeds
2 tsp coriander seeds
$1/3$ cup salted butter
1 tsp ground turmeric
1 tsp black mustard seeds
2 garlic cloves, crushed
2 dried red chilies
$1^1/2$ pounds baby new potatoes

1 Grind the cumin and coriander seeds together in a pestle and mortar or spice grinder. Grinding them fresh like this captures all of the flavor before it has a chance to dry out.

2 Melt the butter gently in a roasting pan and add the turmeric, mustard seeds, garlic and chilies and the ground cumin and coriander seeds. Stir well to combine evenly. Place in a preheated oven at 400°F for 5 minutes.

3 Remove the pan from the oven – the spices should be very fragrant at this stage – and add the potatoes. Stir well, so that the butter and spice mix coats the potatoes completely.

4 Put back in the preheated oven, and bake for 20–25 minutes. Stir occasionally to insure that the potatoes are coated evenly. Test the potatoes with a skewer – if they drop off the end of the skewer when lifted, they are done. Serve immediately.

POTATOES

Baby new potatoes are now available all year round from supermarkets. However, they are not essential for this recipe. Red or white old potatoes can be substituted, cut into 1-inch cubes. You can also try substituting parsnips, carrots or turnips, peeled and cut into 1-inch cubes. Peel 8 ounces pearl onions, and mix in with the vegetables for a tasty variation.

SPICY CAULIFLOWER

This is a perfectly delicious way to serve cauliflower. It is a dry dish so can be enjoyed as a salad or at a picnic, or as an accompaniment to a dhansak or korma.

STEP 1

SERVES 4

1 pound cauliflower, cut into florets
1 tbsp sunflower oil
1 garlic clove
½ tsp turmeric
1 tsp cumin seeds, ground
1 tsp coriander seeds, ground
1 tsp yellow mustard seeds
12 scallions, finely sliced
salt and pepper

1 Blanch the cauliflower in boiling water, drain and set aside. Cauliflower holds a lot of water, which tends to make it too soft, so turn the florets upside-down at this stage, and you will end up with a crisper result.

2 Heat the oil slowly in a large, heavy skillet or wok. Add the garlic clove, turmeric, ground cumin, ground coriander and mustard seeds. Stir well, and cover the pan.

3 When you hear the mustard seeds popping, add the scallions, and stir. Cook for 2 minutes, stirring constantly, to soften them a little. Season to taste.

4 Add the cauliflower, and stir for 3–4 minutes until coated

completely with the spices and thoroughly heated.

5 Remove the garlic clove, and serve immediately.

STEP 2

STEP 3

BABY CAULIFLOWERS

For a weekend feast or a special occasion, this dish looks great made with baby cauliflowers instead of florets. Baby vegetables are more widely available now, and the baby cauliflowers look very appealing on the plate. Peel off most of the outer leaves, leaving a few small ones for decoration. Blanch the baby cauliflowers whole for 4 minutes and drain. Continue as in step 2.

STEP 4

OKRA BHAJI

This is a very mild-tasting, rich curry, which would be an ideal accompaniment to a tomato-based main-course curry.

STEP 3

STEP 4

STEP 5

STEP 6

SERVES 4

1 tbsp sunflower oil
1 tsp black mustard seeds
1 tsp cumin seeds
1 tsp coriander seeds, ground
$^{1}/_{2}$ tsp turmeric
1 green chili, deseeded, finely chopped and
    rinsed
1 red onion, finely sliced
2 garlic cloves, crushed
1 orange bell pepper, finely sliced
1 pound okra pods, trimmed and blanched
1 cup vegetable juice
$^{2}/_{3}$ cup light cream
1 tbsp lemon juice
salt

1 Heat the oil in a wok or large skillet. Add the mustard seeds, and cover the pan until they start to pop. Stir in the cumin seeds, ground coriander, turmeric and chili. Stir until fragrant, about 1 minute.

2 Add the onion, garlic and bell pepper, and cook until soft, about 5 minutes, stirring frequently.

3 Add the okra pods to the pan, and combine all the ingredients thoroughly.

4 Pour in the vegetable juice. Bring to a boil, and cook over a high heat for 5 minutes, stirring occasionally.

5 When most of the liquid has evaporated, check the seasoning.

6 Add the cream. Bring to a boil again, and continue to cook the mixture over a high heat for about 12 minutes until almost dry.

7 Sprinkle over the lemon juice, and serve immediately.

OKRA PODS

Okra pods have a remarkable glutinous quality which, when they are added to curries and casseroles, disperses in the sauce and thickens it wonderfully – and naturally!

28

STEP 1

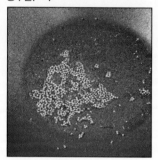

STEP 2

STEP 3

STEP 5

KASHMIRI SPINACH

This is an imaginative way to serve spinach, which adds a little zip to it. It is a very simple dish, which will complement almost any curry.

SERVES 4

1 pound spinach, washed (Swiss chard or baby leaf spinach may be substituted – baby leaf spinach needs no preparation)
2 tbsp mustard oil
¼ tsp garam masala
1 tsp yellow mustard seeds
2 scallions, sliced

1 Remove the tough stalks from the spinach.

2 Heat the mustard oil in a wok or large heavy skillet until it smokes. Add the garam masala and mustard seeds. Cover the pan quickly – you will hear the mustard seeds popping inside.

3 When the popping has ceased, remove the cover, add the scallions, and stir in the spinach until wilted.

4 Continue cooking the spinach, uncovered, over a medium heat for 10–15 minutes, until most of the water has evaporated. If using frozen spinach, it will not need as much cooking – cook it only until most of the water has evaporated.

5 Remove the spinach and scallions with a perforated spoon in order to drain off any remaining liquid. This dish is more pleasant to eat when it is served as dry as possible.

6 Serve immediately while it is piping hot.

MUSTARD OIL

Mustard oil is made from mustard seeds, and is very fiery when raw. However, when it is heated to this smoking stage, it loses a lot of the fire, and takes on a deliciously sweet quality. It is quite common in Asian cuisine, and you should find it in any Indian or oriental store.

ROASTED EGGPLANT CURRY

This is a rich vegetable dish, ideal served with a tandoori chicken and naan bread. Also delicious as a vegetarian dish with rice.

STEP 1

STEP 2

STEP 3

STEP 4

SERVES 6

2 whole eggplants
1 cup natural yogurt
2 cardamom pods
$\frac{1}{2}$ tsp ground turmeric
1 dried red chili
$\frac{1}{2}$ tsp coriander seeds
$\frac{1}{2}$ tsp ground black pepper
1 tsp garam masala
1 clove
2 tbsp sunflower oil
1 onion, sliced lengthwise
2 garlic cloves, crushed
1 tbsp grated gingerroot
6 ripe tomatoes, peeled, deseeded and
    quartered
fresh cilantro to garnish

1 If you have a gas stove, roast the 2 eggplants over a naked flame, turning frequently, until charred and black all over (for other methods see box, right). This should take about 5 minutes. Peel under running cold water. Cut off the stem end, and discard.

2 Put the peeled eggplants into a large bowl, and mash lightly with a fork. Stir in the yogurt. Set aside.

3 Grind together the cardamom pods, turmeric, red chili, coriander seeds, black pepper, garam masala and clove in a large pestle and mortar or spice grinder.

4 Heat the oil in a wok or heavy skillet over a medium heat, and cook the onion, garlic and gingerroot until soft. Add the tomatoes and ground spices, and stir well.

5 Add the eggplant mixture to the pan, and stir well. Cook for 5 minutes over a low heat, stirring constantly, until all the flavors are combined, and some of the liquid has evaporated. Serve immediately, garnished with cilantro.

VARIATION

The eggplants can be cooked over the barbecue, in which case they will char in a shorter time, with frequent turning. Alternatively, they can be cooked in a very hot oven for 15 minutes, turning once, although this method will not give the rich, smoky flavor to the eggplant that makes this dish so distinctive.

CHAPTER THREE

Lentils & Legumes

It is true, in the south of India at least, that Hindus are predominantly vegetarian. In the north they are influenced by their Muslim and Persian neighbors, and more of the northern Hindus eat meat. But wherever you are in India, the meat is not always the tender, succulent product that we have come to expect in the West. This protein source often has to be supplemented, and there is a huge range and variety of lentils – dals – available.

A lot of Indians – and, for that matter, visitors to India – do survive on rice and dal or some sort of lentil stew for days or even weeks. Although it seems an unvaried diet, it is nourishing and quite satisfying. *Thali* is one of the ways in which rice and dal is eaten; it takes its name from the tray that the dish is served on – a round metal tray holding 6 or 7 small metal dishes (*katoris*) around the edge, leaving room for a large pile of rice in the middle. However, in some restaurants a big fresh banana leaf will take the place of the tray. This southern Indian dish will usually have 2 or 3 dals, a curried vegetable, relishes and chutney and a few poppadoms, and they are especially tasty. A *thali* is standard Indian Railway fare, appearing magically fresh and hot as it is served to hundreds of passengers *en route*.

Opposite: *The setting sun illuminates the Lake Palace at Udaipur.*

STEP 1

STEP 2

STEP 3

STEP 4

LONG BEANS WITH TOMATOES

I often feel that Indian meals need some green vegetables to complement the spicy dishes, and to set off the rich sauces. I have created this dish as a side order for tandooris, rogan josh or biryani. It will go with most Indian dishes.

SERVES 4–6

1 pound green beans, cut into 2-inch lengths
2 tbsp ghee
1-inch piece gingerroot, grated
1 garlic clove, crushed
1 tsp turmeric
½ tsp cayenne
1 tsp ground coriander
4 tomatoes, peeled, deseeded and diced
⅔ cup vegetable stock

1 Blanch the beans quickly in boiling water. Drain and refresh under cold running water.

2 Melt the ghee in a large saucepan. Add the grated gingerroot and crushed garlic. Stir and add the turmeric, cayenne and ground coriander. Stir until fragrant, about 1 minute.

3 Add the tomatoes, tossing them until they are thoroughly coated in the spice mix.

4 Add the vegetable stock to the pan. Bring to a boil, and cook over a medium-high heat for 10 minutes, until the sauce has thickened, stirring occasionally.

5 Add the beans. Reduce the heat to medium, and heat for 5 minutes, stirring.

6 Transfer to a serving dish, and serve immediately.

GINGER GRATERS

Ginger graters are an invaluable piece of equipment to have when cooking Indian food. These small flat graters, made of either bamboo or china, can be held directly over the pan while you grate. They have an ingenious way of dealing with gingerroot, which leaves most of the tough stringy bits behind.

STEP 1

STEP 2

STEP 3

STEP 4

MURKHA DAL

With this dal recipe, I wanted to re-create a delicious dal that I ate on my first visit to India. The garlic is intended to burn in the bottom of the pan, and this flavor permeates the dish.

SERVES 4

1/4 cup butter
2 tsp black mustard seeds
1 onion, finely chopped
2 garlic cloves, finely chopped
1 tbsp grated gingerroot
1 tsp turmeric
2 green chilies, deseeded and finely chopped
1 cup red lentils
4 cups water
1 1/4 cups coconut milk
1 tsp salt

1 Melt the butter in a large saucepan over a moderate heat. Add the mustard seeds, and cover the pan. When you can hear the seeds popping, add the onion, garlic and gingerroot. Cook, uncovered, until they are soft and the garlic is brown, about 7–8 minutes.

2 Stir in the turmeric and green chilies and cook for 1–2 minutes until the chilies soften a little.

3 Add the lentils, and cook for 2 minutes, stirring frequently, until the lentils begin to turn translucent.

4 Add the water, coconut milk and salt. Stir well. Bring to a boil, then reduce the heat, and simmer for 40 minutes, or until the desired consistency is reached. You may like it more liquid than I do, in which case 40 minutes will be about right, but cook it for longer if you prefer a thicker consistency. (However, if you intend to reheat the dal later rather than eat it straightaway, cook for only 30 minutes to allow for reheating time.)

5 Serve immediately, while piping hot.

LENTILS

There are many types of lentil used in India, but the two most commonly used are red lentils and green or beige lentils. The red lentils are particularly useful, as they cook in a relatively short time down to a homogeneous mass. The green and beige lentils stay more separate when cooked.

YELLOW SPLIT PEA CASSEROLE

If ever there was a winter warmer, this is it – an intensely satisfying dish, ideal for serving with a lightweight main dish such as pilau or biryani, but equally good with a richer curry and fresh naan bread.

STEP 1

SERVES 6

2 tbsp ghee
1 tsp black mustard seeds
1 onion, finely chopped
2 garlic cloves, crushed
1 carrot, grated
1-inch piece gingerroot, grated
1 green chili, deseeded and finely chopped
1 tbsp tomato paste
1 cup yellow split peas, soaked in water for 2 hours
1 3-ounce can of chopped tomatoes
2 cups vegetable stock
1½ cups cubed pumpkin
8 ounces cauliflower, cut into florets
2 tbsp oil
1 large eggplant, cubed
1 tbsp chopped fresh cilantro
1 tsp garam masala
salt and pepper

1 Melt the ghee over a medium heat in a large pan. Add the mustard seeds, and when they start to splutter, add the onion, garlic, carrot, and gingerroot. Cook until soft, about 5 minutes. Add the green chili, and stir in the tomato paste. Stir in the split peas.

2 Add the tomatoes and stock, and bring to a boil. Season well.

3 Simmer for 40 minutes, stirring occasionally. Add the pumpkin cubes and cauliflower florets, and simmer for an additional 30 minutes, covered, until the split peas are soft.

4 Meanwhile, heat the oil in a skillet over a high heat. Add the eggplant, and stir until sealed on all sides; remove and drain on paper towels.

5 Stir the eggplant into the split pea mixture with the cilantro and garam masala. Check for seasoning.

6 Transfer to a serving dish, and serve immediately.

STEP 2

STEP 3

TIPS

When cooking with lentils and legumes, be sure that you do not over-stir, as this will break up the individual peas or beans.

To transform this recipe into a one-pot meal, simply add some cooked meat such as bacon, lamb or duck.

STEP 4

STEP 2

STEP 3

STEP 4

STEP 5

COOL BEAN SALAD

This is a delicious "Indian Summer" dish, ideal for serving at a barbecue, or to accompany one of the hotter Indian curries, or served as part of a salad buffet at parties – just remember to remove the garlic.

SERVES 4

1 red onion, finely sliced
3 cups fava beans, fresh or frozen
$2/3$ cup natural yogurt
1 tbsp chopped fresh mint
$1/2$ tbsp lemon juice
1 garlic clove, halved
salt and ground white pepper
$1/2$ English cucumber, peeled, halved and
  sliced

1 Rinse the red onion slices briefly under cold running water, and drain well.

2 Put the fava beans into a pan of boiling water, and cook until tender, 8–10 minutes for fresh, 5–6 minutes for frozen. Drain, rinse under the cold tap and drain again.

3 Shell the beans from their white outer shells, and you are left with the sweet green bean. This is optional, but well worth the effort.

4 Combine the yogurt, mint, lemon juice, garlic and seasoning in a small bowl.

5 Combine the onion, cucumber and fava beans. Toss them in the yogurt dressing. Remove the garlic halves.

6 Spoon the salad onto the serving plate.

RAW ONION

I find that rinsing the raw onion under running water takes the edge off the raw taste, as it washes away some of the juices. The same technique can be used on other pungent vegetables and salad, such as scallions, bitter cucumbers and chilies.

STEP 1

STEP 1

STEP 3

STEP 4

KABLI CHANNA SAG

Beans are widely used in India, and this satisfying, earthy dish is characteristically easy to make and quite delicious.

SERVES 6

*generous 1 cup whole garbanzo beans,
    rinsed, soaked overnight and drained*
5 cloves
1-inch piece cinnamon stick
2 garlic cloves
3 tbsp sunflower oil
1 small onion, sliced
3 tbsp lemon juice
1 tsp coriander seeds
2 tomatoes, peeled, deseeded and chopped
*1 pound spinach, rinsed and any tough
    stems removed*
1 tbsp chopped fresh cilantro

TO GARNISH:
fresh cilantro sprigs
lemon slices

1 Put the garbanzo beans into a saucepan with enough water to cover. Add the cloves, cinnamon and 1 whole unpeeled garlic clove that has been lightly crushed with the back of a knife to release the juices. Bring to a boil, then reduce the heat, and simmer for 40–50 minutes, or until the garbanzo beans are tender when tested with a skewer. Skim off any foam that comes to the surface.

2 Meanwhile, heat 1 tablespoon of the oil in a saucepan. Crush the remaining garlic clove. Put this into the pan with the oil and the onion, and cook over a medium heat until soft, about 5 minutes.

3 Remove the cloves, cinnamon and garlic from the pan of garbanzo beans. Drain the garbanzo beans. Using a food processor or a fork, blend $1/2$ cup of the garbanzo beans until smooth with the onion and garlic, the lemon juice and 1 tablespoon of the oil. Stir this purée into the remaining garbanzo beans.

4 Heat the remaining oil in a large skillet. Add the coriander seeds, and stir for 1 minute. Add the tomatoes. Stir and add the spinach. Cover and cook for 1 minute over a medium heat. The spinach should be wilted, but not soggy. Stir in the chopped cilantro and remove from the heat.

5 Transfer the garbanzo beans to a serving dish, and spoon over the spinach. Garnish with the cilantro and lemon.

STEP 1

STEP 2

STEP 3

STEP 4

KITCHOURI

This is the dish from which kedgeree evolved! The traditional breakfast plate of smoked haddock, egg and rice reputedly has its roots in this flavored rice dish, which the English colonists adopted and to which they added preserved fish, to make the version that we know today.

SERVES 4

2 tbsp ghee or butter
1 red onion, finely chopped
1 garlic clove, crushed
$\frac{1}{2}$ celery stalk, finely chopped
1 tsp turmeric
$\frac{1}{2}$ tsp garam masala
1 green chili, deseeded and finely chopped
$\frac{1}{2}$ tsp cumin seeds
1 tbsp chopped fresh cilantro
generous $\frac{1}{2}$ cup basmati rice, rinsed under
    cold water until water runs clear
$\frac{1}{2}$ cup green lentils
$1\frac{1}{4}$ cups vegetable juice
$2\frac{1}{2}$ cups vegetable stock

1 Melt the ghee in a large saucepan. Add the onion, garlic and celery, and cook until soft, about 5 minutes.

2 Add the turmeric, garam masala, green chili, cumin seeds and cilantro. Stir until fragrant over a medium heat, about 1 minute.

3 Add the rice and green lentils, and stir until the rice is translucent, about 1 minute.

4 Pour the vegetable juice and vegetable stock into the saucepan, and bring to a boil. Cover and simmer over a low heat for about 20 minutes, or until the lentils are cooked. They should be tender when pressed between 2 fingers. Stir occasionally.

5 Transfer to a warmed serving dish, and serve immediately.

VEGETARIAN LUNCH

This is a versatile dish, and can be served as a great-tasting and satisfying one-pot meal for a vegetarian. I have also served it as a winter lunch dish with tomatoes and yogurt.

CHAPTER FOUR

Rice & Bread

Rice is a staple ingredient in Indian cooking; it is served at virtually every main meal, and acts as a filling base and a foil for the richer, spicier dishes. The stunning mountain ranges that are the Himalayas provide the crystal-clear mineral water that is used to grow basmati rice. For basmati rice to be classified as such, it must be grown in the foothills of the Himalayas. However, it is such a desirable commodity in the world market that due to "creative" sales techniques more "basmati" rice is sold each year than is harvested! Basmati rice has more perfume than long-grain rice, is whiter, and has a longer grain.

Bread is another staple ingredient, used to mop up sauces and stews, and it makes meals easier to eat with the hands. Indian bread is very easy to make, as it needs very little kneading and rising, and is usually quickly deep-fried or dry-fried. It appears in many forms – pooris, poppadoms, oven-baked naan, pan-fried chapatis and parathas – all equally delicious.

Opposite: Fresh food and other wares are often transported by boat along the backwaters of India.

STEP 1

STEP 2

STEP 3

STEP 5

SAFFRON RICE

This is the classic way to serve rice, paired with saffron, so that each brings out the best in the other. To get maximum flavor from the rice, soak it overnight and drain before cooking. Reduce the cooking time by 3–4 minutes to compensate.

SERVES 8

12 saffron threads, crushed lightly
2 tbsp warm water
1 ³/₄ cups water
8 oz basmati rice
1 tbsp toasted, slivered almonds

1 Put the saffron threads into a bowl with the warm water, and leave for 10 minutes. They need to be crushed before soaking to insure that the maximum flavor and color is extracted at this stage.

2 Put the water and rice into a medium saucepan, and set it over the heat to boil. Add the saffron and saffron water, and stir.

3 Bring back to a slow boil, stir again and let the rice simmer, uncovered, for about 10 minutes, until all the water has been absorbed.

4 Cover tightly, reduce the heat as much as possible, and leave for 10 minutes. Do not remove the lid. This insures that the grains separate, and that the rice is not soggy.

5 Remove from the heat, and transfer to a serving dish. Fork through the rice lightly, and sprinkle on the toasted almonds before serving.

SAFFRON

Saffron is the most ancient of spices, and continues to be the most expensive – literally worth its weight in gold. It is still harvested and sorted by hand, and is a treasured commodity. The purest, strongest saffron – La Mancha grade – is not easily found. Saffron is grown in Europe and the Mideast, and is found worldwide in food and drinks. It is used in England for Cornish saffron cake, in Italy for risotto, in France for bouillabaisse, and in Spain for paella.

Saffron stigmas are wiry, 1 inch long and are a vibrant reddish-orange or sometimes yellow color – the deeper color is the better quality. Powdered saffron may be substituted for the threads. This is usually a very low grade of saffron that has been heavily adulterated. Although it will not give the flavor, it provides a pleasing color, though the dish will lack the extra visual appeal of the threads trailing through the rice.

SHRIMP PILAU

*This is an Arabian-inspired creation, reminiscent of the spice trade of
Sri Lanka. I have served it many times, at family meals, sophisticated
dinner parties and summer buffets, and it has been a hit every time!*

STEP 1

SERVES 4–6

1-inch piece gingerroot, peeled
4 garlic cloves, peeled
3 green chilies, deseeded
1 tsp cumin seeds
2 tsp coriander seeds
2 tbsp oil
2 shallots, finely chopped
generous 1 cup basmati rice
10 cloves
2-inch piece cinnamon stick
5 cardamom pods
1 bay leaf
$\frac{1}{2}$ cup coconut milk
$1\frac{3}{4}$ cups fish stock
1 cup cooked, peeled shrimp
2 tbsp cashew nuts, roughly chopped and
 toasted
2 tbsp chopped fresh cilantro
2 tbsp grated or shredded coconut, toasted

TO GARNISH:
lemon and tomato wedges

1 Grind together the gingerroot,
garlic and chilies in a coffee grinder
or pestle and mortar.

2 Toast the cumin and coriander
seeds, and then grind them also.

3 Heat the oil in a wok or large
skillet. Add the shallots, and cook
over a medium heat until soft, about 5
minutes. Add the garlic mixture, and stir
until fragrant, about 1 minute. Add the
cumin and coriander. Add the rice, and
stir until translucent.

4 Put the cloves, cinnamon,
cardamom and bay leaf into a piece
of cheesecloth. This is not essential, but it
makes them easier to remove at the end.
Add the bag of spices to the pan.

5 Stir in the coconut milk and fish
stock. Bring to a boil, stir once and
simmer for 15–18 minutes, or until all
the liquid is absorbed.

6 Add the shrimp, cashew nuts and
cilantro. Cover with a close-fitting
lid or a piece of foil. Reduce the heat to
the lowest setting, and leave undisturbed
for 10 minutes.

7 Discard the cheesecloth bag of
spices. Transfer the pilau to a
serving dish, and fork through lightly.
Sprinkle over the toasted coconut, and
garnish with the lemon and tomato.

STEP 2

STEP 4

STEP 6

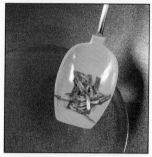

STEP 1

STEP 2

STEP 3

STEP 4

HYDERABAD RICE PILAU

This is a wonderfully colorful and complex pilau, full of spice and flavor and aromatic ingredients, from exotic okra to saffron and hot cayenne. Though it is quite simple to make, it looks very impressive on the dinner table.

SERVES 6

3 tbsp sunflower oil
1 onion, finely sliced
3 shallots, finely chopped
1 garlic clove, crushed
1 tsp grated gingerroot
2 cups basmati rice
$\frac{1}{2}$ tsp cayenne
2 cups okra pods, trimmed
4 cups chicken stock
1 tsp saffron, lightly crushed
rind of $\frac{1}{2}$ orange, with pith shaved off
$\frac{1}{3}$ cup golden raisins
1 tbsp lemon juice

TO GARNISH:
$\frac{1}{4}$ cup slivered almonds, toasted
1 tsp chopped fresh mint
1 tsp chopped fresh cilantro

1 Heat the oil in a wok or large skillet until quite hot. Fry the onions until golden brown, then remove and drain on paper towels. Do not cook them all at once, as they won't be crispy.

2 Reduce the heat under the wok or skillet. Cook the shallots in the remaining oil until soft, about 5 minutes. Add the garlic and gingerroot, and stir. Stir in the rice, cayenne and okra.

3 Pour in the chicken stock, saffron and orange rind. Bring to a boil, and simmer over a medium heat for 15 minutes.

4 Add the golden raisins at the end of this time, and stir in the lemon juice.

5 Remove the piece of orange rind if you prefer, then transfer to a serving dish, and garnish with the fried onion, toasted almonds, mint and cilantro.

RICE

Rice which is labelled "precooked," "pre-fluffed," or "easy cook" has undergone a process that drives some of the vitamin C and minerals back into the grain from the rice husk, a process which also hardens the outside of the rice so that the grains stay separate and fluffy. So never imagine that this rice is inferior – it is in fact far better for you than natural rice!

SPINACH POORI

These little nibbles are very satisfying to make. They are the most attractive green color to start with, and when you fling them into the pan, they start to puff up immediately. Don't be slow in serving them and they will still be little puffballs when you get to the table.

STEP 2

SERVES 6

1 cup whole wheat flour
1 cup all-purpose flour
¹/₂ tsp salt
2 tbsp vegetable oil
¹/₂ cup chopped spinach, fresh or frozen,
    blanched, puréed and all excess water
    squeezed out
¹/₄ cup water
oil for deep-frying

RELISH:
2 tbsp chopped fresh mint
2 tbsp natural yogurt
¹/₂ red onion, sliced and rinsed
¹/₂ tsp cayenne

1 Sift the flours and salt together into a bowl. Drizzle over the oil, and rub in until the mixture resembles fine bread crumbs.

2 Add the spinach and water, and stir in to make a stiff dough. Knead for 10 minutes until smooth.

3 Form the dough into a ball. Put into an oiled bowl, and turn to coat. Cover with plastic wrap, and set aside for 30 minutes.

4 Meanwhile, make the relish. Combine the mint, yogurt and onion. Transfer to a serving bowl, and sift the cayenne over the top.

5 Knead the dough again, and divide into 12 small balls. Remove 1 ball, and keep the rest covered. Roll this ball out into a 5-inch round.

6 Put the oil into a wok or wide skillet to 1-inch depth. Heat it until a haze appears. It must be very hot.

7 Have ready a plate lined with paper towels. Put 1 poori on the surface of the oil – if it sinks, it should rise up immediately and sizzle; if it doesn't, the oil isn't hot enough. Keep the poori submerged in the oil, using a spatula or a perforated spoon. The poori will puff up immediately. Turn it over, and cook the other side for 5–10 seconds.

8 As soon as the poori is cooked, remove and drain. Repeat with the remaining balls of dough.

STEP 4

STEP 5

STEP 7

STEP 6

STEP 7

STEP 7

STEP 9

PESHWARI NAAN

A tandoor oven throws out a ferocious heat; this bread is traditionally cooked on the side wall of the oven where the heat is only slightly less than in the center. For an authentic effect, leave your broiler on for a long time to heat up before the first dough goes on.

SERVES 4–6

1/4 cup warm water
pinch of sugar
1/2 tsp active dried yeast
4 cups strong bread flour
1/2 tsp salt
1/4 cup natural yogurt
2 sharp, green dessert apples, peeled and
  diced
1/3 cup golden raisins
1/2 cup slivered almonds
1 tbsp cilantro leaves
2 tbsp grated coconut

1 Combine the water and sugar in a bowl, and sprinkle over the yeast. Leave for 5–10 minutes, until the yeast has dissolved, and the mixture is foamy.

2 Put the flour and salt into a large bowl, and make a well in the center. Add the yeast mixture and yogurt to the bowl. Draw the flour into the liquid, until all the flour is absorbed. Mix together, adding enough tepid water to form a soft dough, about 2/3 cup.

3 Transfer to a floured board, and knead for 10 minutes until smooth and elastic. Put into an oiled bowl, and cover with a cloth. Leave for 3 hours in a warm place, or in the refrigerator overnight.

4 Line the broiler pan with foil, shiny side up.

5 Put the apples into a saucepan with a little water. Bring to a boil, and mash them down. Reduce the heat, and continue to simmer for 20 minutes, mashing occasionally.

6 Divide the dough into 4 pieces, and roll each piece out to a 8-inch oval.

7 Pull one end out into a teardrop shape, about 1/4 inch thick. Prick all over with a fork.

8 Brush both sides of the bread with oil. Place under a preheated broiler at the highest setting. Cook for 3 minutes, then turn the bread over, and cook for an additional 3 minutes. It should have dark brown spots all over.

9 Spread a teaspoonful of the apple purée all over the bread, then sprinkle over a quarter of the golden raisins, the slivered almonds, the cilantro leaves and the coconut. Repeat with the remaining 3 ovals of dough.

STEP 1

STEP 2

STEP 4

STEP 6

SPICY OVEN BREAD

This is a Western-style bread that I have made Indian, rather than vice versa. It is very quick once the dough is made, which can be left in the refrigerator to rise slowly over a long period – overnight or all day is fine. The bread itself is quite a rich mix and very tasty.

SERVES 8

1/2 tsp active dried yeast
1 1/4 cups warm water
4 cups strong white bread flour
1 tsp salt
1 cup melted and cooled butter
1/2 tsp garam masala
1/2 tsp coriander seeds, ground
1 tsp cumin seeds, ground

1 Mix the yeast with a little of the warm water until it starts to foam and is completely dissolved.

2 Put the flour and salt into a large bowl. Make a well in the center, and add the yeast mixture, and 1/2 cup of the melted butter. Blend the yeast and butter together before drawing in the flour and kneading lightly. Add the water gradually until a firm dough is obtained; you may not need it all.

3 Turn the dough out, and knead until smooth and elastic, about 10 minutes. Put the dough into an oiled bowl, and turn it over so that it is all coated. Cover and leave in a warm place to rise until doubled, about 30 minutes. Alternatively, leave in the refrigerator overnight.

4 Punch down the dough, and divide into 8 balls. Roll each ball out to about a 6-inch round. Put onto a floured baking sheet. Sprinkle with flour, and leave for 20 minutes.

5 Mix the spices together with the remaining melted butter.

6 Brush each bread with the spice and butter mixture, and cover with foil. Place on the middle shelf of a preheated oven at 425°F for 5 minutes. Remove the foil. Brush with the butter once again, and cook for an additional 5 minutes.

7 Remove the bread from the oven, and wrap in a clean dish cloth until ready to eat.

VARIATIONS

Substitute 1 tablespoon saffron threads in 2/3 cup of tepid milk for the spice mixture, and use 1/2 cup of butter. Or substitute 1 teaspoon fennel seeds, 1 teaspoon cumin seeds and 1 teaspoon coriander seeds, ground together, for the spice mixture.

CHAPTER FIVE

Accompaniments

In the Indian subcontinent the heat is often so intense and enveloping that it is essential for every cook to have in his or her repertoire pickle and chutney recipes which preserve a wide range of ingredients regardless of the heat. Salt, oil, vinegar and citric acid can all be used as a means of preserving, depending on the effect that you want.

These preserves have claimed their place in the grand scheme of Indian gastronomy – no table would be complete without a selection of pickles presented on a tray for you to dip into. Who could imagine eating a dry, spicy tandoori dish without a yogurt accompaniment? Or crisp poppadoms without the mango chutney? Not only do Indian pickles and preserves accompany meat and fish, but because vegetarianism is such a way of life in India, they are devised to complement the meat-free meals too.

I have tried here to demonstrate a cross-section of methods and ingredients used in a selection of six accompaniments. Lassi yogurt drink is a delicious way of cooling down a spicy curry, or quenching your thirst on a hot summer's day – it is an essentially Indian and aromatic drink.

Opposite: *Ingredients and cooking utensils being transported by boat on a lake in Kashmir.*

STEP 1: Tomato

STEP 2: Tomato

STEP 3: Tomato

STEP 4: Tomato

TOMATO, ONION & CUCUMBER KACHUMBER

This is a relish that is served at all Indian tables as a palate refresher, or an appetizer, or simply as a relish to garnish the main meal. I have included two variations on the main recipe.

EACH SERVES 6

TOMATO, ONION & CUCUMBER KACHUMBER:
3 ripe tomatoes, peeled
1/4 English cucumber, peeled
1 small onion, quartered
1 tsp lime juice
2 green chilies, deseeded and chopped (optional)

1 Cut the tomatoes into quarters, and cut each quarter in half. The seeds can be removed at this stage, if you prefer.

2 Cut the English cucumber lengthwise into quarters.

3 Remove the seeds from the cucumber, and cut into cubes.

4 Cut each onion quarter into slices.

5 Combine all the ingredients in a bowl, and sprinkle with the lime juice.

6 Add the chilies, if using, and serve.

MANGO KACHUMBER:
1/2 mango, peeled and chopped
1 small onion, chopped
1 tbsp chopped fresh cilantro
2 tomatoes, chopped

1 Combine all the ingredients in a bowl, and serve.

RADISH KACHUMBER:
8 large radishes, sliced
1/2 cucumber, peeled and chopped
1 small onion, chopped
1 tbsp chopped fresh cilantro
1 tbsp oil
1 tbsp vinegar

1 Combine all the ingredients in a bowl, and serve.

PEELING TOMATOES

To peel tomatoes, make a little cross in the bottom of each one with a pointed knife, then place in a bowl, and cover with boiling water. Leave for 1 minute before draining. The skins will slip off easily.

STEP 1: Cucumber

STEP 2: Cucumber

STEP 2: Cucumber

STEP 3: Cucumber

CUCUMBER RAITA

In any Indian restaurant, the first thing to be brought to the table should be a kachumber salad (see page 64) and a raita, which you eat with a few poppadoms while you make a selection from the menu. Here I have suggested three variations in addition to the original recipe.

SERVES 4

CUCUMBER RAITA:
2 tsp fresh mint
½ English cucumber
1 cup natural yogurt
salt and pepper
grated nutmeg to serve

1 Chop the fresh mint finely.

2 Peel the cucumber, and deseed it. Cut into matchsticks.

3 Combine the yogurt, mint and cucumber. Season to taste.

4 Transfer to a serving dish, and sprinkle over nutmeg to serve.

GRAPEFRUIT RAITA:
1 tsp sugar
1 tsp finely grated grapefruit rind
½ grapefruit, segmented
1 cup natural yogurt
salt and pepper

1 Combine all the ingredients and serve immediately. This version should be eaten on the day you make it, as it does not keep for more than a day.

MELON RAITA:
¼ honeydew or firm melon, peeled and cut into ½-inch cubes
¼ medium pineapple, peeled and cut into ½-inch cubes
1 tsp cayenne
1 tsp ground coriander seeds
1 cup natural yogurt
salt and pepper

1 Combine the melon and pineapple cubes, cayenne, ground coriander seeds, and salt and pepper in a bowl. Stir in the yogurt, and serve. This will keep for 1–2 days in the refrigerator.

DATE RAITA:
6 dates, chopped
1 tbsp raisins
1 sharp, green dessert apple, chopped
1 cup natural yogurt
salt and pepper

1 Combine all these ingredients in a bowl, and serve. This will keep for 1–2 days in the refrigerator.

STEP 1

STEP 2

STEP 3

STEP 4

LIME PICKLE

This is the hottest and most thirst-making of the Indian pickles. Ginger pickle is the sweetest, but lime pickle is the one that will have you going back for more!

MAKES ENOUGH FOR 2 x 1 POUND JARS

6 limes, rinsed
½ cup salt
1 tbsp yellow mustard seeds
1 tsp fenugreek seeds
seeds from 2 star anise
4 small green chilies, finely chopped
⅔ cup light muscovado sugar
1 tbsp ground ginger
3–4 tbsp water

1 Cut the limes into quarters. Put them into a wide bowl, and sprinkle over the salt. Leave for 24 hours.

2 Next day, put the mustard seeds, fenugreek, star anise seeds and chilies into a dry saucepan, and cover. Place over a high heat, and roast the spices, shaking the pan constantly until the mustard seeds start to pop. Remove from the heat.

3 Strain the liquid from the limes into a small pan. Add the sugar, ginger and water. Boil for 2 minutes, or until the sugar has dissolved.

4 Combine the limes and spices thoroughly, and put into 2 clean, dry preserving jars. Pour over the sugar mixture, making sure that it covers the limes. If it doesn't, cram the limes further down into the jar, or remove one or two quarters.

5 Cover the jars loosely, and when quite cool, screw on the lids tightly. Label each jar, adding the date on which the pickle was made. Keep for 4 weeks before using.

FENUGREEK

Fenugreek can be bought quite easily in supermarkets and Indian stores. It adds rather a bitter taste to recipes, which is sometimes needed – here I have used it to offset the sweetness of the sugar.

WALNUT CHUTNEY

This delicious fresh chutney is from Kashmir, and would complement the Butterfly Prawns on page 18 beautifully. I have included a variation, Garlic Chutney, for those who prefer a hotter flavor.

STEP 1: Walnut

SERVES 4–6

WALNUT CHUTNEY:
½ cup shelled walnuts
scant 1 cup natural yogurt
2 tbsp chopped fresh cilantro
1 green chili, chopped
1 garlic clove, finely chopped
salt
fresh cilantro sprig to garnish

1 Grind or chop finely in a spice grinder or by hand ¹/₄ cup of the walnuts.

2 Chop the remaining walnuts roughly by hand.

3 Combine the chopped and ground walnuts.

4 Stir in the yogurt, cilantro, chili and garlic. Season to taste. You will find the chutney thickens a lot at this stage. Transfer to a serving dish, and garnish with cilantro. This will keep for 1–2 days in the refrigerator.

GARLIC CHUTNEY:
10 garlic cloves
1 cup raw peanuts
2 tbsp shredded coconut
3 green chilies, chopped
4 tbsp lemon juice
salt
1 tsp ground cumin
1 tsp ground coriander

1 Put all the ingredients into a pestle and mortar or food processor, and grind with enough water to make a paste. Let sit for an hour before serving. This will keep for 1–2 days in the refrigerator.

STEP 2: Walnut

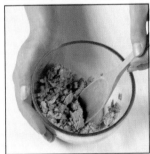

STEP 3: Walnut

WALNUTS

Although this walnut chutney can be made successfully at any time of the year, the flavour will be slightly different, as it tastes best when made with fresh walnuts bought at the height of the season. The same applies to any chutneys and pickles – choose ingredients that are in season for the best results.

STEP 4: Walnut

CHILI CHUTNEY

Surprisingly enough an Indian meal isn't always hot enough for everybody. This chutney will give a bite to the meal, as well as a zingy lime freshener to the palate.

STEP 1

STEP 2

STEP 3

STEP 4

SERVES 6

1 lime, rinsed and halved, very thinly
   sliced
1 tbsp salt
2 red chilies, finely chopped
2 green chilies, finely chopped
1 tbsp white wine vinegar
1 tbsp lemon juice
$\frac{1}{2}$ tsp sugar
2 shallots, finely chopped and rinsed
1 tbsp oil

1 Combine the lime slices and salt. Leave for 30 minutes.

2 Rinse the chilies in the vinegar briefly. Drain.

3 Combine the chilies, lemon juice, sugar, shallots and oil.

4 Stir the salted limes into the other ingredients.

5 Transfer to a non-staining serving dish. Serve with any mild or rich curry.

CHILIES

The outward appearance of a chili is no guide to the heat content: large chilies can be blisteringly hot, and small ones can be sweet and mild, though the reverse is usually true.

There are a number of ways to reduce the heat in chilies. The chili seeds are the hottest part of the chili, so the simplest and most common method is to leave out the seeds altogether. Chilies give up more of their heat when they are chopped, so if you use them whole in the dish and remove them before serving, they will impart less heat to the dish. However, if you do want to slice or chop them, they can be rinsed in cold water before use, which removes a little heat. Rinsing in vinegar removes more. Also, if you blanch chopped chilies in boiling water, you discard the heat with the water.

Above all, use caution – it is easier to increase the heat than to reduce it. The chilies should be added gradually, and the dish tasted at every stage. Some dishes can be "cooled" by extending the simmering time; and if you do overdo it, try eating rice or bread to cool your mouth, as this is more effective than drinking large quantities of water.

STEP 1

STEP 2

STEP 3

STEP 4

LASSI YOGURT DRINK

This is a deliciously fragrant drink that you can easily imagine the maharajas' ladies sipping! The choice of the sweet or savory version is entirely a matter of taste.

SERVES 4

SWEET VERSION:
2¹/₂ cups natural yogurt
2¹/₂ cups water
1 tsp rosewater
4 tsp superfine sugar
4 cardamom pods, crushed, pods discarded
1 tbsp pistachio nuts

SAVORY VERSION:
2¹/₂ cups natural yogurt
2¹/₂ cups water
¹/₄ tsp salt
1 tsp sugar
¹/₄ tsp cumin seeds, ground and roasted
fresh mint sprigs to garnish

1 For both versions, put the yogurt and water in a bowl or jug, and whisk together until smooth.

2 For the sweet version, stir in the rosewater, superfine sugar and cardamom pods. Add more sugar if required. Mix together well.

3 Chop the pistachio nuts. Serve over ice, and decorate with chopped pistachios.

4 For the savory version, stir the salt, sugar and cumin into the yogurt and water.

5 Mix together well. Serve over ice, and garnish with mint sprigs.

ROSEWATER

Rosewater has acquired very romantic connotations, not least because it was precious enough to be offered up to the gods in times past. It is made from the extracts of rose petals, and is not too expensive to buy in small quantities. It is available from good supermarkets, health food stores and delis.

INDIAN COOKING

METHODS AND TECHNIQUES

Some of the methods used by an Indian cook to get the most nutrition and flavor from a wide range of ingredients are completely new to us, while others are very familiar. Indian cuisine differs enormously from area to area, from the cold, mountainous northern region to the dry desert-like land in the south, and has many influences. It is impossible to pin down every method and every technique, so some adaptation is necessary for us to cook these dishes.

Some methods are in any case not suitable for Western kitchens. One recipe for making a lime pickle requires boiling 2$\frac{1}{2}$ cups of oil, and adding an equal quantity of vinegar, which I thought too dangerous to try in the average kitchen and found another way to achieve the same result. I also decided to find a substitute for "stand the bottle in the sun for 15 days, turning once, every day"!

However, to achieve an authentic result, it is important to treat spices and other strong flavors with care. To "stir until fragrant" is to stir over a low heat (unless otherwise stated), until the spices release their flavor; it is important that you do not heat the spices past this point, but carry on immediately with the recipe, otherwise the flavors will become bitter.

THE INDIAN MEAL

If you are fortunate enough to visit India, you might find the typical Indian meal as varied as I did; in Darjeeling, a most colonial resort, we indulged in a meal at a sumptuous hotel – it was very cold outside, but inside the fire was lit, and we could have been in an English country house hotel, had it not been for the menu. Further north, we ate in cubicles curtained off against the cold, where tea was served in a mug with a lid. In the desert we ate on rooftops and courtyards, always under the stars, and the beautiful desert sky. And in Delhi, we had a panoply of restaurants to choose from, including a Wimpy bar (true!), an ice cream parlor, luxury Western hotels and, my favorite, a Southern Indian vegetarian restaurant where we were served paper-thin dosas sculpted into cones 12 inches high.

But whatever the meal, it was always served with an array of complementary dishes – rice, bread, dal, vegetables, and the ubiquitous chutneys and pickles.

Indian flavor

Indian dishes are based on subtle combinations of spices, which are treated in various ways to bring out different flavors. To eat these curries on their own would be enjoyable, but to have the flavors tempered by the rice and bread and contrasted with the dals and vegetables is much more satisfying.

The Indian cook takes a lot of trouble to grind spices, and to heat them in ways to bring out different nuances of flavor, and similarly to balance the main dish with other dishes of different flavor and texture. A bhaji is a dry curry, a sabzia is a sauced curry, and a bhartha is a vegetable purée; you could put a sabzia with a dry tandoori and a kachumber for a tempting combination, or a mild, rich moghlai curry could be combined with rotis and rice and a dry bhaji.

This book provides a wide selection of recipes that are suitable to serve as accompaniments to main-course Indian dishes, and will help you to re-create the experience of an authentic Indian meal, and bring out the best in your Indian cooking. Needless to say, any of the dishes could also be served as snacks and main courses in their own right – just increase the quantities accordingly.

SPICES AND OTHER INGREDIENTS

In the majority of my recipes – with the odd exception – I have written "spices, ground." Once you have tried cooking with spices that you have freshly ground yourself, I am convinced that you will not go back to using ready-ground. The flavors are so fresh and so aromatic that they are not easily forgotten, and will impress all who come to your table. Throughout India, cooks grind their own spices in a mortar and pestle or *sil-vatta*, as they are known there. But here in the West we can have almost the same effect at the press of a button. You can buy a small, inexpensive spice grinder or coffee grinder, which will enable you to make your own freshly ground blends in just a few seconds.

The more practical advantage of using freshly ground spices is that you know that the seeds you grind will taste the same as the seeds that I grind. Ready-ground spices deteriorate very rapidly, and are often adulterated, so there can be vast differences between two separate brands of ground cumin, for example. Grinding your own spices will insure that you get the right results.

Black onion seeds

These are also known as nigella, and the onion seed description is actually inaccurate. The tiny tear-shaped, dull black seeds have a faintly nutty taste. Sometimes described as black cumin (kala jeera) or kalonji.

Cardamom

Also known as elaichi, this is a highly aromatic pod, whether green (more common) or black. It is a very ancient spice, and is rated as precious, along with vanilla and saffron. Either the pods are used whole, or the seeds are extracted to impart their lemony perfume. The cardamom pods are not meant to be swallowed, but can be chewed in order to freshen the breath. Cardamom is reputed to cleanse the digestive system.

Cayenne

This is in fact a particular kind of chili, ground. It is not the same as chili powder, which is often blended with other spices too. It is a very pungent fine red powder which is widely available – delicious with smoked salmon.

Chilies

Chilies are a delicious ingredient, but should be treated with respect. Wash your hands immediately after chopping them, and do not touch your eyes until you have done so.

The finer the chili is chopped, the more heat it gives up – for instance, if a whole chili is used uncut in a dish, it will give up its flavor, but not much heat; cut in half, it will give up more heat; finely chopped, it gives up all its heat. As a general rule, the green chilies are hotter than the red. Add chilies little by little to the dish until the required heat is reached. If you overdo it, soothe your sore mouth with yogurt or rice, which is much more effective than drinking large quantities of water.

Cilantro leaves

These are usually added, chopped, toward the end of cooking so that they lose none of the sweet flavor. It is a flavor that some find too overpowering but once tried, it is never forgotten.

Cinnamon

This is the dried bark of a tree, and has a delicate, sweet woody aroma, which is very warming. The sticks can be ground in a blender or pestle and mortar, but this will take time.

Cloves

These flower buds from an Indonesian tree have a dark rich sharp taste. They are easy to grind into a powder.

Coconut milk

This is not the liquid found inside the

BEANS AND LENTILS

Beans and lentils are many and varied, but almost all need to be soaked before cooking. Drain and rinse them well after soaking; do not cook them in their soaking water as this will contain indigestible substances.

If you wish to experiment with beans or lentils other than those I have used in this book, here are some examples of soaking and cooking times:

Black-eye peas
Soaking time	Cooking time
7–8 hours	1–1 1/2 hours

Garbanzo beans
Soaking time	Cooking time
7–8 hours	1 1/2–3 hours

Navy beans
Soaking time	Cooking time
7–8 hours	1–2 hours

Red lentils
Soaking time	Cooking time
none	20–30 minutes

Green/beige lentils
Soaking time	Cooking time
1 hour	1 hour

Split green/yellow peas
Soaking time	Cooking time
1 hour	45–60 minutes

Whole green/yellow peas
Soaking time	Cooking time
7–8 hours	1–1 1/2 hours

Curry powder
Here is my recipe:

2 dried red chilies
2 tsp coriander seeds
2 tsp cumin seeds
1 tsp yellow mustard seeds
1 tsp cardamom seeds
8 cloves
1 × 3-inch cinnamon stick
1 tsp ground ginger
1 tsp ground turmeric

Heat all the ingredients slowly in a dry skillet. Grind together to a fine powder, and store in an airtight jar.

Garam masala
This is a blend of spices which each cook will make up to his or her own recipe and grind, to keep in an airtight jar, and use when required. The recipe I have used is this:

1 tsp cardamom seeds
2 tsp cloves
2 tbsp cumin seeds
2 tbsp coriander seeds
2 bay leaves
1 × 3-inch cinnamon stick
1 tbsp black pepper

coconut, but is made from the pressed flesh of the coconut. It is available in canned and powdered form from larger supermarkets and Asian stores. It is very rich, and should be used in moderation, but it is a delicious addition to cold drinks such as pineapple juice.

Coriander seeds
These are one of the most widely used spices in Indian cuisine. They are used whole for pickling, and for myriad other uses in their ground form. Both Indian and Moroccan coriander seeds can be bought; the Indian type is slightly more elongated than the Moroccan round seed and, I think, more fragrant.

Cumin seeds
These are widely used in Indian cuisine, usually in their ground form, but in some bhajis you will find them whole. The seeds are long and thick; when ground, they impart a sweet smoky flavor.

Curry powder
In authentic Indian cooking, curry powder is freshly ground by the cook at home, to an individual recipe. See left-hand column for my recipe, which you can vary according to your own taste.

Fennel seeds
These are long thin seeds, pale green in color. They have a sweet aniseed flavor, and are usually used whole. It is these seeds that you may be presented with at the end of an Indian meal in order to freshen your breath and digest your food. Very pleasant to chew.

Fenugreek
These dull mustard-yellow seeds are irregular in shape, but similar in size. They are also known as methi, and have a very bitter taste when ground, but this is sometimes required in an Indian recipe to balance the other, richer spices.

Garlic
Sweet cloves of garlic add another dimension to any dish, though people are often put off using them because of the way the smell lingers. If the garlic clove is crushed and added to the dish, the aroma will linger; however, there are other ways to use garlic. I find that if the clove is added whole or halved and allowed to infuse the sauce, the flavor is not so pungent. Also, cooking oil can be flavored with garlic, and the oil retains a mild flavor after the garlic is removed.

Ghee
This is Indian clarified butter that has been separated and the sediment removed. It is long-lasting, and is usually sold in cans.

Gram flour
This is garbanzo bean flour, and has special qualities that make it useful as a thickener in Indian cooking and in batters for deep-frying. It can be bought in Asian stores, but can also be made from dried garbanzo beans. These must be lightly crushed before grinding, otherwise the mill blades will break on the rock-like garbanzo beans.

Mustard oil
This is never used raw. On heating, the

hot pungent mustard flavor is replaced by a unique sweet aroma that is the basis of many curries. It enhances green vegetables, such as kashmiri spinach, like nothing else. The great advantage to using mustard oil in Indian cuisine is that pickles made with this ingredient never seem to go off or lose their flavor. It is sold in all Asian stores, and is worth looking for, but if it is not available, substitute rapeseed oil.

Mustard seeds
Yellow and black mustard seeds release their flavor when split or crushed, and the easiest way to do this is to put them into a hot pan with a lid, and listen to them explode before adding the remaining ingredients. Mustard seeds have a hot, sweet aroma.

Nutmeg
Grated nutmeg gives a rich, almost creamy, nutty flavor to a variety of dishes. The outer lacy coating of nutmeg is mace, which has a similar flavor to nutmeg, only slightly more bitter.

Paprika
This is an orange-red powder, similar in appearance to cayenne, but it has a sweeter flavor. It is made in Hungary by grinding special varieties of sweet bell peppers, and is said to have been taken there by the Turks. Hungarian paprika is the best quality to buy, and is widely available nowadays. Paprika is probably the quickest of the spices to lose its pungency. When it starts to go brown, the flavor has gone.

Rosewater
Rosewater does indeed taste and smell of roses, and is made from extracts of rose petals. It is inexpensive, and is widely available in supermarkets and health-food stores.

Saffron
One of the most ancient of spices and the subject of many a clash on the high seas, saffron has been traded and treasured for thousands of years. This featherweight spice has an aroma and color like none other. It may seem expensive, but a little goes a very long way.

Star anise
This is the most decorative of the spices, and is used in its whole or ground form. The seeds are sometimes used by themselves. It has an aniseed–liquorice taste which complements fish well, as well as leeks and onions.

Turmeric
This is the root of a plant, and is very rarely seen in its whole state. It is usually sold ground, and used for its dense musky flavor as well as its strong golden yellow color. It is reputed to have antiseptic properties.

Zucchini flowers
These have a delicious and distinctive nutty flavor. You will find them in some vegetable markets, usually sold singly, wrapped and sometimes still attached to the baby zucchini, which can be cooked in the same recipe. The flower is large and yellow, with a center stamen, which should be removed before cooking.

INDIAN BREAD
Most Indian breads are quick and easy to make, as the dough needs little or no rising or kneading, as is common in breadmaking, and the bread is cooked quickly over a high heat. The dough ingredients can vary; they always consist of flour and water and usually ghee, and yeast is sometimes used. But after that, a variety of ingredients can be kneaded into the dough, such as yogurt, vegetables, potatoes and, of course, spices.

The four breads below are the most common kinds of Indian bread:

Chapatis are thin rounds of bread made of flour, water and ghee. They are cooked in a dry skillet, then held over a flame for a few seconds to puff up and blacken slightly.

Pooris are thick, puffy rounds of bread usually made with flour, yeast, water and ghee. The dough is kneaded and risen, filled with some kind of filling, then fried.

Parathas are similar to pooris, but slightly flatter. The dough is made of flour, water and ghee, and is brushed with ghee before being folded and fried.

Naan bread is a large teardrop-shaped bread, made with flour, water and yeast. The dough is broiled under a very hot broiler.

INDEX